Perspectives

*Poems
by
Judith Rycroft*

Carol dear,

You are a wonderful friend, I am so grateful for you!

love, Judith

ACKNOWLEDGMENTS

Thanks to the editors of journals
where several of these poems first appeared—
Diplomatic Service Wives' Association Newsletter
Pegasus of Rose State College
New Plains Review of UCO
Red Dirt Press

Artwork and Design for book cover, section pages
and pen and ink drawing "Caltofts"
by Nicki Rycroft
Pencil Sketch "A Daughter at Ten"
by Judith Rycroft
Graphic Files by Margaret Gaeddert
Publisher: Cathy Miller

Happy Dance Press

ISBN: 978-1-7329487-7-8

This collection of poems
is lovingly dedicated to

Carl Sennhenn,

teacher, editor, mentor, friend.

THANKS

Thanks and gratitude to my reviewers
Debra Blakely
Colleen Perry
Audrey Streetman
Connie Greaser
Nicki Rycroft
Sandra Soli

and to the excellent feedback and support from
Carl Sennhenn's Creative Writing workshop at
Rose State; my critique group NDYP; "Zoomba
Poetry" friends
Kathy Bass
Julane Borth
Cathy Miller
Emily Tullos Simms
Audrey Streetman;
and Creative Project Management by Cathy Miller.

Finally, special thanks to Connie Greaser, who
tirelessly edited and advised, and to my wonderful
illustrator and constant editor, Nicki Rycroft.

Distance and time alter perspectives—
mountains become molehills;
years absorb shadows of the past.

TABLE OF CONTENTS

I. REFLECTIONS

II. VIEW FROM THE HEART

III. OUR WORLD

IV. LOOKING BACK

V. IMAGES

VI. WHIMSY

VII. CONVERGENCES

VIII. A BIT ABOUT ME

REFLECTIONS

PERSPECTIVES

Points of perspective
expand to contain
both circumstance and change,
alpha in omega, distance and time,
elastic connections.

Life in retrospect is the comfort
of the elderly. Reflections of the past
lay color on contemplations of the future,
give clarity or impinge upon decisions
of today, fill the gaps of distance.

Separation is amplified when
we lay our longings across space
as yardsticks rather than as vibrations
of those ties which must not bind
and cannot be severed.

Reunions always glisten with tears
but miles and days have no dominion
within a unison of souls.
Love can be measured
both in moments and millenniums

and horizons are only
points of perspective.

SHARED WORDS

Your children...come through you but not from you....
You may house their bodies but not their souls, for
their souls dwell in the house of tomorrow.
                        —*Kahlil Gibran,* The Prophet

We seek to guide our children,
give them the language of wisdom
condensed into words—
words not wholly of truth,
for prisms of thought cast their color in patterns
shaped by the surface they touch.

We strive to share our own experiences,
but not to limit a child's explorations of his world,
to suggest a better path, but never to direct each step
for our words are nestling creatures meant someday
to fly on winged notes of understanding.

We observe our children edge into maturity
less governed by our dictates and more
by the guidance of an open mind and sense of self.
We wish them acceptance of themselves
with the same tolerance they allow others.

If our words are chosen wisely,
our children will know right from wrong,
not by edicts of society nor constraints of law,
but by listening to whispers of conscience.

We guide our children with words
plucked from the vaulted chambers of our hearts,
set down as lyrics in a song of love,
so they might someday find within that melody
the notes of their own glad songs of being.

I REMEMBER

In the cooling shade of my 80+ years
I bask in the warmth of memories.
They swirl and meld, to form my present Self.
I close my eyes, the better to see
beloved images, vignettes—

of my mother
  in bright coordinated colors,
  captivating her students
  sitting at her piano in a purple blouse
  long fingers on the keys, those same hands
  growing liver-spotted and arthritic, playing on;

my father
  in his workshop building, repairing, inventing,
  professor, designer, dreamer,
  letters, poetry across the miles and years,
  his tears at the loss

my daughter through the years,
  her first steps, barefoot, red dress,
  arms and smile wide, ponytail with tangles
  only her father could dislodge,
  her favorite stuffed toy, called *Pachyderm,*
  reluctant world traveler, tears and laughter
  writer, artist, philosopher, seeker of stability.

Once wanderlust withered my Oklahoma roots,
created a sharp and clear present which itself
has now faded at the edges.

Yet...love is the glue
that binds the years when the past
threatens to dart out of reach—
and I remember love.

SEEDS

I had a tomato for breakfast.
I opened it with my little knife,
curved blade, black handle
serrated edge—best
for broaching outer resistance.

I stared at the opened fruit,
red flesh protecting
viscous insulation for tiny seeds
destined never to grow,
like the half-million eggs
my young body held in waiting.

Where are you, my unborn children.
I used to hear you call to me
but your voices have been stilled.
In the mystical magical workings
of the human body, I absorbed you.
You lie silent in the memories
of my aging cells.

Tomato seeds
run down my chin.

BENT

I remember
when I could bend
any direction—
back bends, lotus position.

I could rise
from lying prone
without using hands
—mine or anyone's.

Once I could even bend
my understanding
of the world to reach a core
of good intentions in bad acts.

I remember being proud
of being American, bending credulity
to allow conviction of the basic goodness
of my country's leaders.

In the stiffness of age
my balance and belief
totter on unyielding joints
and mankind's absurdities.

I cower in the danger zones
of time, knowing all too well
that those who cannot bend
will break.

HARK

To know life
listen

to a newborn's
first cry

a couple's
I do's

the dying breath
of an old soul

soft taps of rain
on trembling leaves.

Life whispers
a constant song

to those
who hear.

A DAUGHTER AT TEN

There's a hopeful touch of borning
in the drearest, wettest morning,
there's a sun among the rain clouds
all the while;
There's a moon-and-starry brightness
in the deepest type of nightness
in the presence or the memory
of her smile.

There's a constant conversation
of compassion and elation,
there's a youth-belying knowing,
somehow wise;
There's a silent song of living,
of receiving love and giving
in the dancing depths and freshets
of her eyes.

LINGERING SCENT

Mohi from Iran
had caramel-colored skin,
soft eyes
like melted Bakers' Chocolate,
exotic cologne
reminiscent of sandalwood
and honeysuckle.

He wrote me love poems in Farsi,
whispered Khayyam in my ear,
taught me to admire the Baha'i faith,
said I must marry him
or he would surely die.

When I hear the word "Iran,"
I do not think of conflicts,
oil, or nuclear bombs.
I think of soft brown eyes,
The Rubáiyát,
a haunting scent.

PETALS

Daffodils bloom on my little dog's grave.
Beside the mound
Jane Magnolia grows strong and high,
croons a song to near spring.
Her tight green buds open

in a miracle of blossom.
Ivory hands, blush-tipped,
cup a nestled sea anemone,
crimson arms raised
to the sun.

Flowers droop under rain drops,
quiver in the wind,
scatter petals on the ground
to blanket new grass from
dying winter's cold fingers.

If my ashes are scattered here
someday I will be a petal on the ground
—become a part
of the eternal
cycle of life.

BLOOD

According to the Law, all things are cleansed
with blood, and without shedding of blood
there is no forgiveness.
                              —Hebrews 9:22

India roiled in unrest
riots and war
but I was safe in my hotel
during an overnight layover.

Morning brought sounds of drums,
shouts. From my window I could see
the street filling. *What's happening?*
I asked the manager.

It is a parade of Shia Muslims
for Ashura. They cut themselves
to mourn the death of Hussain,
the Prophet Muhammad's grandson.

I started out to the street to watch
but was stopped. *Memsahib, you cannot go.*
It is not good you see, too dangerous
for white lady!

I thanked him, returned to my room
got my camera, and went up to the roof
where I hid behind the air conditioning unit.
and watched the parade.

The street was packed--hundreds of men
in frantic flagellation, swinging
chains with razor-sharp knives on the end
to slice their brown backs, now patterned red.

Thrum of drums, stomp of feet
cries of pain, shouts
of *Ya Hussain,* and everywhere
blood, blood, blood.

There's heathen blood
all over the street, said the English woman
at dinner. I replied, *We Christians*
also revere the shedding of blood.

Jesus' hands and feet on the cross, stigmata,
in hymns 'There is a fountain filled with blood,'
'Just as I am…Thy blood was shed for me,'
in Communion 'Drink. This is my blood.'

There are no heathens,
only worlds we do not know.
All religions worship through symbols.
Blood symbolizes the essence of life.

FURRY REQUIEM

Time can be measured in moments of love,
in snuggles and wags of their tails.
We grow used to their sounds—
the clink of their tags,
the click on the floor of their nails.

If we sometimes are grumpy or late with their food,
one pat will make them forget.
When we leave them alone for an hour or a day
they worry and watch and fret.

We know we can't keep them forever
—a decade more or less;
but when they leave us, we long for the chance
of one more sweet hug or caress.

When the light in those trusting eyes grows dim,
when their joy begins to fade,
we must let them go with a kiss, despite
our wish that they could have stayed.

We remember how much they brightened our days,
dry our tears, and offer a prayer
that, if Heaven is all it's cracked up to be,
our friends will be waiting there.

BELIEFS

Having seen the unbelievable
accepted the inexplicable
heard the impossible
my belief system is an open book
with unfilled pages.

Irredeemably imprinted
by my Baptist upbringing,
still, I have seen dancing lights
in Norwegian snow drifts,
heard crescendos of choral music
in midnight Irish woods,
been told truths by an Isphahani seer,
loved my Hindu, Brahman, Buddhist,
Muslim, Sikh, agnostic friends,
known miracles of healing,
found comfort in the Catholic mass.

Beliefs grounded in love,
tolerance, respect for the teachings,
reverence for Omniscient Power,
these are added to my book.
I do not dispute the names of other gods
only seek to defend all hearts
filled with compassionate faith.

TOO WHITE

I am a white woman
whose voice is drowned
in the roiling waters of
systemic racism.

My cries of outrage
and encouragement
hit the frothing surface
and sink without ripples.

Reactions of the oppressed
who hear the echoes of my cry
range from *Thank you, Ma'am,*
but you just can't know

to a sneer at the intrusion
of this pale skin, which is no more
a matter of embryonic choice
than dark skin.

I have known pain, but not your pain.
I can't walk in your shoes, but
take my hand and I'll walk beside.
Compassion should have no color.

HEY GOD

This morning,
looking up through the boneyard
of bare winter branches
against a heavy gray sky,
I called softly,
Hey God, are You up there?

In Sunday School classes,
more than seven decades ago,
I had been assured
that He was, in fact, up there,
always watching me.

Heaven has become a dream
to which I cling, and I know
that the sparrow and I are watched.
Yet God is no longer "up there"
but within me, a part of my being.

I hear Him
in the prayers of a child,
in joyful hymns, in the chant
of ritual, in cries of the hopeless
and the pulse of ventilators.

I see Him
in a new mother's eyes.
in tiny buds on broken trees
in a grandmother's smile behind the glass

I feel Him
in the whisper of colored leaves
and when daffodils bloom in the snow.

SOLITARY REFLECTIONS

In this isolation I lose sight of self
as old friends and family disappear
from my life one by one.
Through thoughts of the past,
I bring them back.
Those images close the doors
on subtle threats around me.

Morning sky brightens
in pinks and blues.
I pour through albums and files,
not stopping to drink the wonder
of a dawning day. The dust I brush
from pictures hanging in the hall
mixes with smiles and tears.

At noon, as the sun uncurls petals
on the dahlias. I am immersed
in piles of yellowed journals
seeking the forgotten.
Stress slips away
as I recall the joys
of a former day.

Later, when the western sky
shoots phosphorescent orange
through the tulip tree,
I sit at my computer, weaving stories
from the tangled threads
of ancient memories.

In this endless isolation
I have lost today.

SWATTER THOUGHTS

In this moment of waiting
for the fly to land
I wonder
how many designated minutes
of my life
have I squandered
waiting for the perfect instant
to act.

If lost time
accumulated,
lay within my next step,
could I change the world—
my little world,
my tiny storehouse of words,
ideas, random acts...

or would I,
like the fly,
step unaware
into oblivion.

View

from

the
heart

MASTERPIECE

I used to long to touch the Pietà—
the flowing solidity of such smoothness
would surely teach my touch
all that could be learned of
the feel of beauty.

That was before my hands explored
the lifewarm curves and crevices
of your living masterpiece.

WHITE WHITE THE FRANGIPANI

Stark white against the night
the Frangipani blooms.
Poinciana-silhouette upon a citylight-lit sky,
glorycolor of day enveloped in nighttime's
black, white and gray.

I can never see or smell or touch
those gold-based perfect blossoms
without thoughts of you, Richard.
White petals, your long hands,
our little girl bedecked in leis—
blonde beauty Frangipani framed.

Black and deep, my husband's eyes,
warm and white the blossom. His smile
above our Nicki's head returns to me.
Pikake dreams, white-ginger-tinged,
bring memories of such strength
they cut across the years, reach me
at midnight on the veranda,
as this tropical night wraps me in fragrance.

I feel
my lost love's presence, see his brush,
suspended, the half-completed canvas
collecting dust.

I remember
a hospital at night, waiting
with the unsharability of gut deep pain,
a fear that words might render real
magnified by silence. Back then I stood,
with you but alone, void of your pain
which could no longer touch you,
void of expectancy because I *knew*.

I ran my fingers through your hair,
the side that wasn't swathed,
slipped the sapphire from your hand to mine,
touched your cheek, walked to the door,
not looking back. You were no longer there.
That is when we three became two.

The nightguard struggles stiffly to his feet,
stretches, prepares to walk his last duty round
unaware of my presence.
Somewhere in the silence
a morning bird bursts into song.
I stir, aware that it is not the proper thing
to sit with scent of Frangipani
in communion with the past.

I have felt your filling presence
in the walled-up dusty chambers
of my disillusioned soul. Now
I will sleep, awake to noonday sun
and solitary reality.

Stark white against the night
is love.

KNOW ME

Press your ear to my memory
and hear the music of the past,
paeans of joy,
crescendos of discovery,
the keening of grief.

Once I hid from a tropical storm
that swept my little island clean.
You weren't there,
but press your ear to my memories
and listen to the scream
of wind, the screech
of metal, the silence
of the eye
of the storm.

Brush your lips across my cheek
to taste the salt of tears.
See the scars on my body.
Each welted ridge,
each fine white line
is a chapter of my history—
an expurgated version
because you cannot see
the scars upon my soul.

Hear me,
taste me,
see me.
I want you to understand
who I am
but you aren't here.
You are not here.

JUST ANOTHER LOVE POEM

Love is an imperfect emotion
like the heart's other afflictions,
kaleidoscopic, never static—

a river
flowing, bursting over rocks,
sparkling with sundrops,
darkening under grey clouds,
reflective and tranquil
in channel pools

a desert
vast, shimmering with heat
until night draws its chill blanket,
humming with rustles of the unknown,
barren, then dazzling with color
after rain.

Imperfection is the spice of life—
love's flavors sometimes burn,
always season.

PERHAPS

Some moment will you turn to me and find
no pleasure in the touch or in the sight
of love? Could you lay all these days behind
the armor of your heart? Perhaps you might.

Some morning when I reach to touch your cheek
in awe of beauty, will you turn away
and build a wall of silence while I speak
and let your eyes grow cold? Perhaps you may.

Then someday will you choose to walk alone—
someday, before my love has had its fill?
Before the last day's farewell hours have flown,
will you have said good-bye? Perhaps you will.

I have known this heartbreak once before
and lived to love perhaps a little more.

IN FEAR OF LIFE

In fear of Life I shunned her joy
and dove into a sea
of loss and sank beneath the waves
of harsh reality.

I could not bear a world in which
you were no longer there.
With you absented from my side
I swam in deep despair.

The brine that closed above my head
was made of my own tears.
Alone, a shapeless manatee,
I wallowed in my fears.

Before, in all things, we were one.
Now my bisected self
sank, bankrupted, in the gloom,
bereft of love's vast wealth

The octopi of misery
wrapped tight around my heart.
I drifted over coral reefs
That slashed my soul apart.

Life and I were enemies.
I could not reconcile
the nights without your warming touch
or days without your smile.

Today, the shell I have become
sits static in the flow
of aimless hours and loneliness.
Life will not let me go.

MARRIAGE

Been married—twice.
Certificates no guarantee
of love, longevity,
fidelity, compatibility,
joy.

Mores of our culture
require official
couple-ing.
Legal lock on property
comes with the deal.

Family expectations
no longer bind me.
I've no need
of property or extra
paperwork.

I need the constancy
of devotion. Warm arms
wrapped around my aging body.
Dreams of tomorrow
together.

STAY

Stay still, my heart.
Do not awake
and beat the cadence of the night.
No arms are near to draw you close
and dim the threat of morning light.

Stay dead, my hopes.
Do not revive
and seek to rise to meet the day.
The dawn is lonely, cold and bleak,
and sheets the sun with shades of gray.

Stay mute, my soul.
Do not sing out
and strive to hear a harmony
within the strains of life's refrain
and love's discordant melody.

CLIMATE CHANGE

Love is a hot tropic
riding on the seventh wave
to foam around my heartstrings
and suck the ground out
from beneath. I fall
splayed upon warm sand
in a glistened night, look up
where palm fronds shred the moon
to quivering sequins scattered
on the ripples of the bay.

At dawn a horizontal line of light
separates the sky and sea, dulls the glow
of phosphorescent footprints
we left upon the sand. Brainfever bird
awakes the dawn with shrill orgasmic call
and we smile, content to add another day
to the liturgy of love,

share delight in every breath and sight—
the scent of sweet Pikake, a breeze
that carries hints of burning charcoal,
spices, brine, ellipses of fallen flame tree buds,
red accents on white sand. On the hill
a temple bell sets swallows
into swirling flight.

These winter evenings, house-bound,
I lie curled around such memories,
hold a shell to my ear, remember the sea.
Emotion's flame sputters in the chill of today.
Did it fade with the years, or is this
love's climate change.

GET OUT OF MY DREAMS

I'm past the point of fantasy,
of what-if's, regrets and grief.
You are firmly lodged in my catalog
of memories, pages tabbed to special moments
for my sometime daytime thoughts.

You are history, the past, a road once traveled—
my present self has learned to walk alone.

Stay out of my dreams. Leave
that space of uninhibited imaginings
to young minds, dark nights, strangers,
to goals I never reached, to fears
and impossible acts I can easily forget.

Get out of my dreams. Return
to that photograph on the wall,
that poem,
that story,
that yellowed journal.

To dream of you re-lights the path
I stumbled down to Goodbye.

CALL ME A CYNIC

Forever
and ever
hallelujah hallelujah
Forever is a promise—
a pledge, a hope, a dream,
a postage stamp.

Forever
serves only the moment,
is temporal,
begins in desire
and ends with death
or boredom.

Forever is hollow
It echoes from the walls
of change, longing, human frailties,
deception, of our desperation
to believe in our own immortality
and truth in vows.

Forever is a Siren's song—
Beware.

MOONRISE

I'll sing you a lay of the summer's day
and chant of the falling rain;
but I'll whisper the tune of the month's full moon
in my soul-song's soft refrain.

Softly, softly, hear me sing
while the cloud-bruised sky grows dull;
and listen, my love, to the raindrops ring
In the hush of the twilight's lull.

Gentle genesis of night
in a smoke-pink circle swell—
loose-knit gauze still pricked with light
in a dusk-dim silent spell.

Slowly, slowly, watch it rise
from the arms of the rain-washed tree
till it catches the gold of the western skies
and the last of the sun-streaks flee.

Moon-flecked shadows stir and sigh,
dark branches writhe and twist;
and the leaf-patterned topaz evening eye
spins in the valley's mist.

Come with me, two hearts in flight,
on a race to the edge of the dawn
on a wisp of yellowed, tree-touched light
till the moon and the mist are gone.

I'll sing you a lay of the summer's day
and chant of the falling rain;
but I'll whisper the tune of the month's full moon
in my soul-song's soft refrain.

SEPARATION

Go
Don't Go
Stay
Don't stay—

I spin in the vortex
of love
that rejects
as it pleads for return.

Only a word, unintended,
can spark the flame that
spews hate into clouds that distort
the gentleness and burn the edges of love.

We cannot be together
for that flame has eaten
into my soul, and I cannot
allow this destruction of Self—

Yours and Mine, not Ours.

SO LONG AGO

Tonight a full moon casts patterns
through the willow. Dark shapes
on the terrace shift and dance
like the shadow puppets we watched
at the Diwali festival so long ago.

How quickly
our Known World vanished
that full moon night in Agra
as the Taj Mahal glimmered gold.

We stood, hand in hand,
caught in a reverent silence.
Even the tree frogs muted
their soprano arpeggios.

I remember you lifted
one long gentle finger
to touch the tear on my cheek

pulled me closer, murmured
Shah Jahan's love
was no greater than mine.

So long ago.

VIEWPOINT

She says
she feels like a church,
all stained
glass windows.

To me
she feels like a cloister,
a tempo soothing mind stroke,
the soft slap of leather soled
sandals on stone slabs,
Sanctuary.

TROPICAL FAREWELL

Footsteps beside mine in the surf
        soft rain
        sunset
        purple sky

Voices that span the night
        surf roll
        frond song
        child's night cry

Laughter, tenderness, and tears
        love full
        silence
        sweet goodbye

HERE IS LOVE

Grief is an alteration of who we once were.
It is an adjustment of ourselves, an adaptation
to our souls....Grief is love with no place to go.
                                    —*Kathy Parker*

When

the North Star fades
behind wildfire smoke,
nature bends and breaks
beneath a burden of ice,
thousands flush with fever,
fight for breath, fall victim
to a stealthy virus,

integrity leaks away
in tweets and turmoil,
city streets become battlegrounds
with lives lost in protest,
Democracy faces Armageddon,

we grieve.

Love which makes the sun rise
searches for a lifeline,
flounders in the waves of loss,
of discontent, seeks a foothold
for beauty to return,
trust and brotherhood to rise
from bitter ashes—
for the world to breathe again.

Love will find new direction,
rebuild a home for hope,
a harbor for aching hearts.

STRANDED

Whisper covert thoughts in my ear
in rasping words that cut through
the undercover rustle—
secrets slithering
through synapses
with the click-snap
of an ignition switch.

File your petition in my heart
but leave no footprints in the dust
of disillusion, ground
by days of waiting,
hope ablaze, until a vestige
of cool sanity extinguishes
hot emotion.

Plead your case in logic's court.
Convince the jury locked behind
blue floes of indifference
that you had cause to leave,
to strand our love
among the land mines
of endless solitude.

Our world

WONDROUS

We will raise this wounded
world into a wondrous one.
—Amanda Gorman

It's time
to be wondrous.
The exhaustion of fear
has muted the soul's morning song
too long.

A TIME OF TEARS

Sad is...
a world that is full of fear
an entire nation cowed.
Sad is the absence of someone dear
a loss that echoes loud.

Sad is frustration unreconciled—
the angry ones' excuse.
Sad is the home-bound innocent child
who cannot escape abuse.

Sad is the business with much to lose,
sad is a dying man's moan,
a funeral held to empty pews.
So sad is a lover alone.

Sad is a tear, a sigh, despair,
a feeling that solitude breeds.
Sometimes it fades with a smile or a prayer
but still, this sadness proceeds.

Someday our doors will open again,
we can lay aside our concern
remove our masks, embrace our friends...
Someday life will return.

SAND AND FIRE

In this oasis carved out of sand
cups of bougainvillea cradle morning sun.
Deep wells pipe water, houses drink,
spit out effluvia. Recycled,
it hydrates golf courses, fountains,
kaleidoscope of flowers, acres of green,
whole families of palms.

Hot thirsty sand presses against the gates.

Brilliance of blossom, sun,
blank sheet of blue sky smudged
by puffs of gray creeping
over the mountains from the west
where wildfires rage.

Hot thirsty flames ravage the arid landscape.

Nature lashes her tail,
ignites intruders, explodes in trees,
on roofs, creeps onto manicured lawns.
At the edge of danger a chestnut mare
breaks away from the rope
leading her to safety, turns back
into the smoke.

Crackles of flame, thud of hooves.
She follows the whinny of a frightened foal,
wheels, leads him and three stable mates
back to the men, trucks—deliverance.

Nature is our mother, our provider,
our destroyer—what we take
she avenges.

GOLDEN LAMP— *LAMPARA DORADA*

Still they come
in this enlightened 21st century
through porous borders
in search of a life, relief
from past miseries. In the lands of their birth
the present trembles with deaths,
threats, poverty, fear.

They come on foot, mile
after weary mile, desperate
to glimpse the golden light
at the end of their tunnel
of mindless misery
as they march, plod,
ride and swim.

Many fall prey to coyotes' promises.
They sell everything
even Abuela's gold wedding ring
for a tiny space in the steaming
van that bounces over ruts
on back roads in the circuitous route
to *El Norte*.

Nightmares, dreams,
realities of dusk and dawn--
Their ragged edges overlay the hours
in undistinguishable layers.

Suddenly a siren, a shuddering halt,
Coyote screams *¡Corre! ¡Ve rapido!*
Run! Fast!
Abuela, alone in her denuded hut,
rocks in time to her song of grief——
¿Dónde están mis pequeños, mis bonitas?
¿Dónde está la vida para una anciana?
Where are my little ones, my pretty ones?
Where is life for an old lady?

FALLING LEAVES

Falling leaves in February—
Strange to see the flutter rush
of silhouetted shapes
long past the time
of winter's grasp upon the trees.
A flurry in the morning sun
sweeps past in tumbled haste
then rises, turns, and climbs
currents of wind above the trees.

I stand hand up
to shade my eyes
like scouts of old
above the valley.
I feel no rush of wind,
see no carpeting of leaves
but hear the twittered chorus
of a multitude of swallows
in ecstasy of flight.

THREE TANKAS

Fall

Golden leaves cover
circle of chrysanthemums
blooming this cold day.
Naked branches pray for Spring.
With frost breath I pray for you.

Summer

Hum of cicadas
is summer's song. Leaves rustle
under gentle breeze
that ripples reflections where
pond water heats in the sun.

Wind

Desert metronomes—
palm trees etched on swirling sky
bend, sway, left and right,
dance to Coachella winds,
sweep the heavens clean of cloud.

SUMMER HAIKUS

i
Winter left her mark.
Bare bones of leafless laurel
tremble in July.

ii
Winter's tears dry in
the beauty of summer's blaze.
Sunshine heals torn souls.

iii
Tiny striped lizard
flicks long blue tail, ignores me—
spies a fly nearby.

iv
Bare arms hold appeal
for thirsty mosquitos—I'm
part of the food chain.

v
Summer fires flame high.
Cedars sprung from dark red earth
explode like fireworks.

vi
Proud green climbs the fence
quivers in its innocence.
It's only a weed.

DROUGHT

Before the rain
broke through the heat
sparce grass shriveled,
lay in golden shavings.
Bare earth opened
its mouth. Lips
chapped, hardened
under the sun.

Six Jersey cows
sheltered under wide oak arms
ruminating bran and hay
as their udders swelled.
Two Palominos
shared the shade, stood
nose to tail, hips cocked,
long tails a-twitch.

Ten acres of corn
in tight humped rows
felt their roots begin to curl,
the chlorophyll bleach out.
Leaves drooped
in yellow resignation.
On the section line, Red Cedars
dropped needles, felt no pain.

Life quivered on the edge of death
by fire or thirst. Farmers stood
in noonday sun, prayed for redemption,
brown cheeks slack. Reddened eyes
searched a white-hot sky

before the rain came.

LAMENT

Long leaves of gold adorn the ground
beneath the Corkscrew Willow tree.
Crescendos of incessant sounds
—cicada, bird, and honeybee—

fill the shimmering August air.
Flowers bloom and days are long.
Even in the moon-full night
mockingbird sings a midnight song.

So why do you weep, my willow tree
beneath the stars and summer sun?
Why do you drop your golden tears
before the autumn has begun?

I die of thirst, the willow cries.
My roots are parched and sere
My home is by the riverside
But fate has brought me here.

Picnics love a cloudless day.
At threats of storm, many complain,
but water is the elixir of life
and willows wither without the rain.

THE SCREAM OF NATURE

You know this fellow.
Since his copyright expired
and his title shortened
he's been used, abused,
and fused into logos, ads,
films. This brought him
fame in an eerie way
and fortune at Sotheby's
auction house.

I know this fellow,
met him years ago
in Norway, stood before him
and listened for echoes
to ricochet down the years
but heard no more
than the men behind,
who turned their backs
unmindful
of the chaos in the fjord,
the swirling blood in the sky.

He screamed a warning
more than a century ago.
Do we heed?
Even now, even now
Are we listening?

FLYING SOUTH

Tonight an Oklahoma wind
seeks to strangle the green, rip
coming color from bent branches.
We cower behind insulated walls,
listen to the chimney megaphone
rumble its magnified threats.

Morning does not break
but slowly lifts one corner
of a blanket of heavy cloud
which has suffocated the sunrise,
unravels in the heavy air,
darkens pavements.

Chill wind sings summer's death song,
extinguishes the flash of fireflies,
crumples flower petals, spews
green pecans across the lawn.
Only Chickadee, indomitable,
dares a darting visit to the feeder.

A week ago, shrill locusts
deafened the chatter of squirrels,
the last mow of summer felled
sprigs of green, shaved browning turf,
released the fragrance of cut grass,
hot dust, honeysuckle, and memory.

When south wind touched my face,
shadows in the drizzled rain
promised sun beyond the showers.
Now teeth of the north gnaw
my spine. Shoulder muscles tighten,
prepare for flight—my winter migration.

WAR'S CHILDREN

Eyes of children measure war
in length of village streets
laid waste by combat boots,
in width of rubble
where once stood their homes.
Heat and smoke brand an epitaph
upon the violet morning.

Hunger chews the stomach,
starvation gnaws the bones,
sucks the juice. Blood
that flows from fathers' throats,
grandmothers' hands and feet,
between their sisters' legs
fills the children's dreams.

The rabid bite of war dogs foams
in the children's veins, spreads,
relights the fire. Young survivors learn
the power of their hands—power to pull
the trigger, pin, steel wires,
and nobody, not even the dead,
has such unfeeling hands.

From across the seas come offers
to adopt. Beware.
These are no longer children, and nothing,
not even your love, can heal such wounds
or dull the red of remembering,
for the future has no promise
as bright as blood.

ONCE...A SEAGULL

From the bank above the Sound,
I cast my baited hook.
It arced above the ripples
but on its downward flight
a blur of grey swooped,
caught, lifted into the air
and my reel whined, unwinding.

The rod bowed with tension
on the line, which played out,
ended with a jerk as a gull
fluttered down. I began to wind in,
thinking the bird would shake loose,
but it fought the pull, screamed
in anger or despair.

From nowhere three white gulls circled,
landed on the shore. I lifted
the struggling bird, held its wings
to its side as it fluttered and cried.
Four more, then five, gray and white
Glaucous-winged Gulls encircled my head.
I feared an attack.

Instead, they landed, took up watchful positions
in a semi-circle, while I tucked my catch
under my arm and examined her mouth,
pierced by my hook. The air split in a cacophony
of gull-shriek. For a moment I thought
of cutting the line, freeing the bird
to fly away to probable death.

She looked at me with her dark eyes,
lay calm against my side. Her gray feathers
told me she was a juvenile—a silly teenager
in trouble. Gently I worked at the hook, expecting
sharp beaks from the assemblage to hit my head,
my arms, but the adults twitched and sang
and watched.

When at last the hook was out
with little damage to the web of her beak,
I held the young gull out in my hands.
For a moment she rested, her eyes on me,
then she lifted into the air, immediately surrounded
by her noisy guard-flock. Had they acknowledged
I was not the enemy—does instinct
recognize necessity?

LOSS

Words fade with repetition
and cannot describe this sorrow.
Tears are my voice. Eyes flood
and even the sunrise stalls
caught on an unprepared horizon.

There must be joy
in knowing his pain has ended,
that breath withheld
from drowning lungs now flows
along rivers of peace.

There should be joy
in the knowledge that his sunrise
has thrown off its shackles,
shattered the blackness
of untenable hope.

I grieve for him, for myself
robbed of his presence.
Memories shadow beneath a cowl of regret
that my prayers had not the strength
to interfere with destiny.

I bow my head. Songs
of a midnight mockingbird
punctuate the passing
of his soul.

A FUTURE OF FEAR

Those who have heard
the blast of bombs
the rumble of tornados
the thud of bullets
the scream of a child

know the moment
when time and breath stop
the gut liquifies
in an instant
of paralytic disbelief.

In the aftermath emotions flare—
shock, despair, anger,
a helpless, hopeless withering
of incentive to rise from
literal or figurative ashes.

The devastation of sorrow
bores into the heart
digging a well of grief.
Those whose life is spared
never completely forget.

They face a new reality
in which fear has found
a forever home in echoes
of remembered sounds,
memories, dreams.

Looking Back

CHILDHOOD TABOOS

A sandwich of Miracle Whip
on Wonder Bread
Putting my hand out the car window
to feel the wind through my fingers
Going barefoot
Using bad language
like "butt" and "pee"
Blowing paper boats
across the still waters
of the Baptistry
Sneaking into a side room
after church to drink
all the leftover Welch's Grape
from the little communion glasses
Reading comic books
Listening to Country Music
Sunday movie matinees
Horror films
Grapevine and grass cigarettes
Hiding in the hall closet to listen
to the adults' jokes and stories
Wearing Mother's Sunday watch
to school
Drinking milk from the carton
Disappearing into the bathroom
at dishwashing time
Dancing
Catholics...

I wonder why
my adult self has problems
with indecisiveness.

SALONOPHOBIA

When I was five and facing first grade,
Mother took me to the salon.
For hours I sat under rollers and wires,
horrible smells, heat, and fear
of execution while Mother cajoled
and mopped my tears with Kleenex
and promises of school day stardom
with beautiful hair.

When the rollers came off
and the brush came out,
my fried curls fell to the floor.

I bow in belated gratitude
to Toni, wherever she may be,
for the years of home permanents
that saved me from the salon
and gave me curls that not even a dip
in the horse tank was able to quench.

Until my teens, I spent Saturday nights
clutched by my mother's knees
as she arranged my hair's wet locks
and stabbed me with "bobby pins."

Nightly pin-ups are part of my past.
"Product" shapes and settles my hair
but I'm forced to seek more expert help
when my shaggy mop needs cutting.

I hate to walk into the hair salon...
I'm grown, but my hair remembers.

SNOW DAY

In a previous century
for one glorious day
I was the most popular kid
in the neighborhood.

Fluffy white clouds
dropped out of the sky,
filled our yards, packed
the streets with snow.

Daddy screwed hardware
to an old barn door, attached
my pinto pony Sugar with a harness
she had never worn before

and drove the marvelous sled
to our front door. My brother
and I squealed with delight,
hopped on for a glorious ride.

Sugar clopped up and down
those white Edmond streets,
as children deserted their snowmen,
jumped onto the magical sleigh.

Snow crunched beneath runners,
cheeks pinked in the brush
of cold air, riders laughed and shouted
to parents watching from porches.

Indelible joy! I never paused to wonder
how my sweet professor father
acquired a barn door or convinced Sugar
to be a draft horse for a day.

LILAC

Pearl purple buds in swollen pods
pushed through the leaflets' maze
when the lilac in our garden donned
its "Welcome, Springtime" haze,
the backdrop for this image of
my far-off childhood days.

On Mothers' Day, in Sunday best
—how clear the memory—
Daddy, with his Pentax, posed
my mother, Jim, and me
to photograph a thrice of smiles
beside the lilac tree.

Long years ago...now all are gone
parents, brother, tree.
Fragments of that distant day
are caught in Time's debris—
the scent of lilac blooms in spring
old photographs
and me.

SURPRISES

Hold out your hands
and close your eyes
and I'll give you something
to make you wise
My family's mantra
to introduce a surprise—

puppy, party dress, bright jewelry,
report card, tiny pink seashell,
even a letter of college acceptance.

Hold out your hands and close your eyes...
An exercise not only in excitement
but in teaching trust.

I'll give you something to make you wise...
What wisdom lies in surprise?
The ability to trust is a facet of wisdom,
but as a child I never worried
how a new hair bow, cookie,
or shiny quarter could make me wise.

Older me knows
some wisdom may be achieved
by closing one's eyes
to the intrusions of the present,
but opening them to the unexpected
sparks a thrill through the sternum,
a twist to the gut,
an extra beat
to the heart.

DOUBLE FEATURE

When I was twelve years old
I gave up Saturday afternoon movies.
Not even Flash Gordon
could save me from the dangers
that flowed around the silver screen.

On Saturday afternoons
in the movies, men come
and pass an empty seat to take
the one beside. They wriggle
in their raincoats. Their eyes,
like minnows in a pool,
dart and hover, checking out
possibilities.

One hand is deep inside a pocket.
The other covers mouth and nose
to hide the ragged breath
that punctuates the soundtrack
as the raincoat rustles.
What is it about shame
the mouth wants to conceal?

His leg touches mine, a pressure
plied so slyly that I think perhaps
it is only my imagination,
like Mother said. I grip
my bag of popcorn and gaze
in desperate concentration
at the screen.

Once,
pushed into unfamiliar courage,
I blurted, *Stop that!*

The people in the row behind
said *Hush!* The raincoat man
revealed his mouth
and looked at me
with cold and level eyes.
Stop what?

He went home with me
inside my head
and stared at me
through nightmares.

I didn't tell the manager
because who'd believe a kid?
Child molesters
hadn't even been invented.

Those raincoat men
with minnow eyes and heavy breath…
I used to wonder if they were
somebody's daddy.

ALLEYS

I am lost in the back alleys
of reflection.

Summer heat of childhood
didn't bother me
when I was walnut brown
and free to roam
the curving creek bed.

A trickle was enough
to feed Johnson grass,
sumac, persimmon, pin oak.
Mesquite grew
where the gully opened
to a tumble of sandstone.

Sometimes I caught
a horny toad, stroked his head
until he lay still in my hand.
Hours of work on soft stone
with a fragment of brown glass
left my initials for the ages.

August freedom was doomed
to end in a new school year,
but no classroom held
promise as bright
as sun on a sandstone rock.

The phone reminds me
of duties and responsibilities
on the Main Streets of my days.
Regretfully I exit
time's back alleys.

WELL DONE, JUDITH

Seven feet tall and the pinnacle of authority,
Headmistress M.M. Evans was the personified symbol
of Sherwood School for Girls in the English Midlands.

The high point of my adolescence began
at the end of my twelfth year when I became
a Sherwood Girl. I delighted in every aspect
of my British school--the uniform,
the rules, the rigidity of purpose
all under Miss Evans' omniscient eye.

She was firm of jaw and hand, lean and tall,
not the seven feet my younger self perceived
but a colossus who wore command
like a perfectly tailored garment.
In the microcosm of pubescent girls
she was the pole star guiding us
to decorum, diligence and thrift.

Life bore no greater reward
than Miss Evans' *Well done!* For this prize
I changed my style of writing, studied
until even my parents worried,
memorized all 144 stanzas
of *The Rime of the Ancient Mariner,*
threw my unathletic body into furious games
of field hockey, rounders, and netball.

Miss Evans' words of praise, *Well done, Judith,*
were complete compensation for my efforts,
like a Nobel prize for Bible Drills
a gold medal in Marble Olympics...
like a greeting at the Golden Gate.

#1 FAN

My mother loved my poetry.
She was only one of a fan club
comprised of friends and relatives
who wept and smiled over my lifeblood
words and cosmetic images.
Like Edna St. Vincent Millay!
they used to say, and I was proud
because I didn't know Edna was dead
and virtually buried.

My early poetry survives in limited edition,
faded leaves, and aging ashes of song,
cultivated by my mother's taste, flowered
with phrases snipped fresh or full blown
from an English garden, weighted
with Dickensian diction.

That poetry was the well-shaped,
modestly contained body of my emotions,
corseted in abstractions, draped
in diaphanous philosophy, laxative
and sometimes cathartic—
unlike the pieces I produce now.
These are more solid, more concrete,
rather constipated, unloved by Mother.

Someday I must capture another
tinkling symbol for her pleasure.

CALLOUS

I remember the time we died
with laughter over our granny's pain
when she dropped the pan
of boiling eggs on the kitchen floor.
Hot water rose into the air—
a geyser hung suspended
for a moment in which life
and sound and consequence
took pause, and yes, I still remember

the time we died with laughter when
the pint or so of water landed
in a plash that soaked our Nana's
slippered feet and made her
dance away. We two, inured
to sympathy by the callousness of youth
giggled as she wrapped some ice
in her starched and spotless apron
while red infused her cheeks.

And we...do you remember how we
tried to hide our grins and concentrated
on our plates, where one limp
buttered piece of toast lay patiently
in wait for breakfast egg and Nana said
*Just take your plates and go
sit on the steps,* and I remember
the taste of cold butter
and embarrassment
as we sat eating
outside.

NAÏVE

After only a few months of marriage
we were quite surprised to learn
I was pregnant. We rushed out and bought
Dr. Spock's 1958 Edition of *Baby and Child Care.*

These days there are classes, ultrasounds,
Google answers and tweets, but decades ago
it seemed the world believed that having a baby
was a natural event, largely dependent
on genetic memory. Dr. Spock, in his eagerness
to get to *Child Care,* had little to say about pregnancy.
I had to rely on my doctor.

Take one of these pills every day,
Dr. Payne (yes—Payne!) instructed.
*Take it with the blue side up if you want a boy
and the pink side up for a girl.*

Hubby and I considered, decided it might be nice
to start with a boy, so I took the pills religiously
blue side up. When I went into labor,
Dr. Payne did a manual examination. *Oh yes,
there's his head—a fine boy just waiting to come out!*
So, considering the pills and that pronouncement,
I think I could be forgiven for shouting *IT'S A BOY!*
as I was wheeled, semi-anesthetized, out of Delivery.

Richard, who had seen our new-born,
came to sit beside my bed. He finally convinced me
that our baby was a girl. *Do you mind?*
I asked anxiously, noting the concern on his face.

*No! Actually I'm thrilled, because we have
too many boys in my family...but Darling,
I want you to be strong, because we'll handle this
together; and we'll love her however this turns out.*

I started to panic. *What's wrong?! What's wrong with our baby?!!*

Well, it's her head—she's beautiful, really she is—but...

WHAT? Tell me!

...her head, it's a little deformed.

DEFORMED! How?

It's, uh, sort of...pointed.

No one had told us that a baby's head
often changes shape on the trip
through a tight passage.

We took our perfect little undeformed girl home,
and I rarely consulted Spock, who suggested
Consider hiring a housekeeper for a few weeks.
On a teacher's salary?

I skipped the section about safe padding
for a bassinet——Nicki spent her first few weeks
swaddled in the bottom drawer
of our clothes chest. Spock's later editions
are quite specific about car seats, but Nicki
safely traveled miles in a laundry basket.

Despite these deprivations
our daughter survived, thrived,
brought us untold delight.

Thank goodness the pills got it wrong!

OSTRICH GAME

I used to be American
and knew that, as a former pioneer,
I could handle any beleaguered attack
which marriage to an Englishman
might bring.

I learned the language
spoke it like a native...
of somewhere else,

studied the rules of etiquette
and crooked my little finger
when I held the China cup
that emptied in my lap,

changed my holidays and holydays
ignored Thanksgiving and 4th of July
and forgot to call at the Ambassador's
to sign the book
on the birthday of the Queen,

remembered to serve three wines
to dampen every course
but once served rice and no potatoes
with the meal.

I got by with it because
I was expected to be a little strange
since I was foreign,
but
where I went wrong
was in the ostrich game.

This is a move my Englishman made
in times of crisis or great emotion.
He'd isolate disturbing thoughts
before they had a chance
to crash the barrier of stiff upper lip
and run out through the mouth.
Ostrich-like, he'd plunge
his head into the sand.

Born and bred to verbalize
I met my Waterloo
in that ostrich game.
I never learned to communicate
with tail feathers.

CORNWALL: MAY DAY CELEBRATION

Tintagel Castle on Trevose Head in Cornwall,
England, is one of the most spectacular historic
sites in Britain. Its association with King Arthur
makes it also one of the most famous.

The 'Obby 'Oss festival at Padstow dates from May
of 1803, featuring a Maypole dance and a raucous
and rollicking parade of a hobby horse and its
retinue. The 'Oss consists of a round frame set on a
dancer's shoulders, and covered in black oilskin,
with a small horse's head with a snapping jaw in
the front. It is led by an individual known as the
Teaser, dressed in white and carrying a painted
club. The procession also contains a retinue of
white-clad girls called Mayers playing accordions,
melodeons and drums, and singing,
"... For summer is acome ...."

We walked on the cliff, being blown by the sea
and we, who were foreign to headlands like these,
thought it wondrous that small native flora could be
secure on the cliff face and firm in the breeze.

The morning began with wind-chilled rain
beating down on Tintagel on our first day.
Spring broke anew by each road, each lane.
The slate of the sky and the stone could not gray
the heart-filling sight of young leaf buds unfurled
in a gorse-brightened, daisy-filled, primrose world.

At the site of the castle, perhaps it was meet
for the ruins to be sea-misted, hazy, surreal.
If this place knew the tread of King Arthur's feet
it was better to sit, to listen, to feel,
and to wonder at Time's whispered secrets that lie
in the shadow of Now. The next day, blue sky

sparkled on Padstow. The town filled at dawn
with colors and sounds and holiday gloss
and laughter of revelers, laid upon
the boom-ba-boom of the *'Oss! 'Oss! 'Oss!*
as it swung and stepped to the Teaser's time
and insistent tune of the Mayday rhyme.

Decked in cowslips and bluebells, Mayers danced,
around the Pole in virginal white
while, through the streets the 'Oss wove and pranced.
We were caught in the mood of this ancient rite
but retired at sunset and slept through the thrum
of the rib-shaking thunder of chanting and drum.

CALTOFTS

I intended to die there
in our Forever Home,
steeped in history,
a perfect retreat.

Like most who roam the world
we recognized that someday
we'd stop, settle, grow old, so we began
a search for the perfect property.

Intrigued by an ad we saw in the *Times*
we drove 100 miles from our London flat
into the heart of East Anglia, Norfolk,
dotted with Norman Churches and windmills
whose sails revolved slowly in the breeze
or drooped in disrepair.

Harleston seemed to be a typical English village
--pub, church, greengrocer, butcher, iron monger,
all within a block of the property we viewed.
Across from The Swan Public House, tall hedges
rose in parentheses around iron gates that opened
to the grounds of Caltofts, a magnificent manor house
rebuilt in the 1800s after the original 17th Century
timber mansion was partially destroyed by fire.

Caltofts stood deserted and proud, bordered
by brambles and an eight-foot brick wall draped
in prickly wild roses. Swallows darted from the
stables, figs ripened by the door, and ancient yews
gave shade. We had found our retirement home.

Over the years Caltofts bloomed.
We beat back the brambles, cleared brush from
the pond where I watched Moor Hens and their
chicks. A Cambridge professor told us that our

little lake was a remnant of the 11th C. moat of a
former castle. I wondered what lay in the depths.

On moonlit nights, in the shadow
of Caltoft's tall chimneys,
I heard whispers of Cavaliers
and the snort and stomp of restless horses.

Restoration of the house and crumbling stables
became more and more expensive. Since the property
was on the list of Historical Houses, we had to use
original materials, such as pantiles for the roof,
and mud and wattle—latticed wood strips covered
with a mixture of clay, straw, and dung
on the walls.

Then, one night in a rainstorm,
the 300-year-old brick wall separating Caltofts
from the public lane crumbled. Replacement
would cost thousands. We were forced to sell.

That was another life, another me.
I'll have to find
someplace else
to die.

THE FIRST TIME

Red and yellow, black and white
They are precious in His sight.
Jesus loves the little children of the world.
  —*C. Herbert Woolston*

Imprinted by years of Sunday School,
singing to a picture of Blonde Jesus
smiling at the multi-national children
gathered around Him, I grew up unprejudiced,
ignorant, unexposed to discrimination.

Visiting America, after years
enmeshed in British culture and lingo
—*Tea? One lump or two? Coffee?*
Black or white? Top-up, Dearie?—
I was Greyhounding through relatives
spread from California to Florida.
At a bus-stop in the Deep South
I stood in line to order. My turn came.
A doughnut and white coffee, please.

The server, a middle-aged African American,
drew herself up, eyes pinning me
with daggers of contempt—*Lady,*
we serves black and white from de same pot!
She wheeled to serve the next customer,
leaving me to stutter an unheard apology.
The first time
I was seen
as a bigot…
the memory makes me cringe.

MIDNIGHT IN THE GARDEN OF PHALLUSES

Sometimes my monk and I would stroll
through the grounds of Wat Pho,
Bangkok's largest and oldest Buddhist temple.
As we passed, Thais bowed their heads
in the reverent gesture called a wai,
palms together, like a child in prayer,
fingertips at forehead level.

I frequently visited this Buddhist priest,
enjoying his curiosity about my life,
his explanations about his.
On one of our walks we paused by columns
of varying sizes, most above my head,
their widths encircled by long chiffon scarves.
and women on their knees around the plinths.

*These man-parts represent good luck
but also creation of life,* Phra Poon said.
Knowing I longed for a son, he arranged
for me to meet him on the next full-moon night.
Bring the cloth to tie here, he reminded me.

So there I was, in midnight moonlight,
both arms around a huge stone phallus,
trying to focus on my purpose.
I wrapped my scarf, if not my faith,
around the tall cool pillar, thanked my monk,
and went home to await the advent of my son.

Buddha, like God,
did not answer my prayer.

REMEMBERING WILMA MANKILLER

The times, they were a-changing.
Back in 1985, in Tahlequah Oklahoma
the new chief of the Cherokee Nation
was installed--Wilma Mankiller,
the first female to hold this position.

Newspapers reported
that the new head
of the second-largest Indian tribe,
68,000 strong, "...wore a black suit
and carried a Bible."

My imagination longed for a little pomp
and play-it-on-the-tom-tom ceremony.
In my mind I saw Big Chief Wilma,
eagle-bonneted and leather-fringed,
red toenails hidden by her beaded moccasins.

In that tree climbing, cap-pistol packing,
bow and arrow made of sycamore and string,
always a squaw, never the Chief, part of my mind
I saw her, Mankiller, stand before the teepee council,
head and cheekbone high in tomahawkish splendor.

Hot damn, the woman made
every tomboy's dream
come true!

ATTITUDE ADJUSTMENT

The south end of the second floor
of Old North Tower in Edmond
held our rowdy Social Studies class
in the "Demonstration School,"
taught by unimposing Mr. Howell,
copper skinned and heavy-set.

The spitballs landed like arrows on his back.
I could see how deeply they had pierced
when he turned from writing on the board
to view his sixth-grade class. His sad brown glance
lingered on the smirking boys
slouched in the window row.

I have arranged a field trip
to the town where I grew up, he said.
You will have the chance to see
Oklahoma history and tradition
where bands of my Pawnee Nation
gather for their ceremony.

A noisy bus ride brought us to the site,
where we sat in squirming anticipation
under a chaperone's watchful eye
while our teacher excused himself
...to make some preparations.

Five tribal elders and one young brave
sat around the tall fat drum
and lifted their leather-knobbed sticks.
BOOM boom boom boom shook the air
in unison with their song,
and the Grand Entry began,

with jingle and stomp of moccasined feet,
beads and paint and porcupine quills,
scalp locks and braids, color and swirls.
At the front, in headdress of feathers
and horns, majestic in ritual garb,
strode the Chief of the Pawnee Nation.

We children, of an age
who knew of Indians
only what Saturday movies conveyed,
sat transfixed at the sight
of our unassuming teacher
leading the procession.

Erect and proud, cloaked
in somber dignity, he sat with warriors
standing guard and the Shaman at his side.
Dancers twirled and we, wide-eyed,
whispered in awe, then fell silent
under the brief brown glance
of The Chief.

ENCOUNTER

Casinos fill with a pall of smoke,
cacophony of bells, bongs, shrill
jangles shouting *Jackpot!*,
screams of joy, muttered curses.

In the midst of insanity, a minute figure sits alone,
feet dangling from the tall chair
at the Spanish 21 table. She speaks
with tiny brown hands, waves for hits,
stacks her bets, fingers red and white chips,
all with unchanging expression
while the garrulous dealer chats happily on,
calling cards, wins, losses.

Her face is familiar to me from paintings,
photographs, tours...some Asian tribe,
maybe Lahu? Hmong? from the opium poppy hills
between Thailand and Burma. She is an anomaly
in wool knit cap, black trench coat, Nike sneakers,
chipped fire engine red nails, yet a Hill Tribe smock
under the coat flashes bright triangles of color
from the distinctive hand-sewn border.
No make-up smooths the weathered skin,
carved jade decorates her ears, gold rings
cluster on her right hand.

Fascinated, I watch her, although twice
her black eyes throw suspicious glances at me.
I want only to say *Sawadee-ka*, to tell her
that I find her beautiful, to say how I admire
the character in her face, so like the dried apple
doll of my childhood...but when she turns
on the stool to stare,
I move on.

FORECAST

Years ago, when I was young,
specifically, nineteen,
I met a charming old lady
who told me I was a poet.

On a graduate fellowship
at the University of Arkansas,
I fell into conversation at a faculty reception
with a woman who said, *Call me Rosa!*

On hearing that I wrote poetry,
she invited me to bring my poems
and come to her house for tea.
That night, I didn't realize

that she was Rosa Marinoni,
Poet Laureate of Arkansas,
internationally known and published.
I knew only that her black eyes sparkled,

she radiated warmth, and I felt
honored to receive her invitation.
Through the weeks, over thin china cups
and my ragged manuscripts,

she said my poetry was *eccellente*,
reminiscent of the Greats,
that I must, I really must, publish a book
—and I did.

It took me only 61 years.

GEORGE GARMAN

He resembled nothing so much as a frog,
but no princess appeared
to save him with a kiss.

George Garman was unattractive, flabby,
lumbering, effeminately grandiose of gesture,
with protruding jowls and puffed throat which
punctuated his speech with a sound
like a marriage of adenoidal wheeze and
glottal stop.   I remember

the hours we spent in his small office,
George at his book-strewn desk, I
at a small typewriter table against the wall.
Afternoons were work hours for me,
a naive freshman, part time English Department
secretary at the university. He made me

his sounding board, pouring out
his hopes, fears, his passionate love
of the sound, shape, depth and connotations
of words, the music of poetry, the many voices
of prose—words spoken, words written,
words collected in volumes. He revered

books. Their combination of words
into ideas and images was his truest measure
of the evolution of intellect. To own books,
to be surrounded by them, was the greatest richness
he sought. His mission as a teacher was to help
his students see the incredible beauty
of the classics. The word on campus was that
any male could pass his class with a smile

and by addressing him with the unearned
title of "Doctor." I resented their snickers,
felt almost protective. He seemed
to regard me as a friend, one who listened
without reproof to his secrets and longings.
For the first time in my short life
I heard the taboo word spoken aloud—
"HO-mo-SEX-you-all." I learned

that medication to quell desire
caused weight-gain and lack of focus.
I learned that the public restrooms
were trysting places. I learned, much later,
that George's firing was, ostensibly,
not due to his love of boys but to his being
caught stealing books. The years passed

as George moved from state to state,
college to smaller college, and finally
to a rest home. I heard that he had died,
so was surprised when his Christmas card
caught up with me overseas. *My life,*
he wrote, *has not come to a place of joy;*
but I am sustained by fond memories
of dear, dear friends, as you have always been
to me. I wept.

JUDITH THE UNSUNG

You have never heard my name.
That is as it should be
for mine is the story
of my mistress, Judith,
handmaiden of God,
savior of Israel,
more beautiful and clever
than King David's Abigail.

Our High Priest and the Council
called her *the glory of Jerusalem,*
the great pride of Israel,
and yet our own people
have removed her
from the Sacred Book.

Our outpost village was besieged.
If the Assyrian army got past us
Jerusalem and the Temple
were doomed. After 35 days
without water or supplies the townspeople
pressured our Magistrates to surrender.
My mistress chided them for their lack
of faith. *Open the gates,* she demanded.
I will go to the Assyrians.

Judith and I, for I would not let her
go alone, prepared our souls with prayer,
our bodies with sweet oils, fine jewelry,
festival clothing of the richest quality.
At the enemy camp my mistress
promised to lead the army to Jerusalem
with no loss of life. Her words and her beauty
took us straight to General Holofernes' tent.

There, Judith reclined on lambskins,
flattered the General, plied him with drink.
Beguiled and besotted with lust and wine
he fell back onto his couch in a stupor.
Judith sang a prayer, lifted the General's sword,
and with two blows cut off his head.

I waited at the tent door
as Judith wrapped Holofernes' head
in the jeweled canopy from his bed.
We walked past the guards,
saying we were going to the spring
to pray and bathe. Back up the mountain,
Judith shouted to our people
to open the gates.

What rejoicing, what dancing,
what celebration and sacrifices
to God, who guided Judith's hand.
Seeing their general's head
the Assyrians were routed
and the Temple was secured.

Thus Judith saved Israel
in no less an act of bravery
than when David slew Goliath,
yet David became King
and my beautiful mistress
is lost in the dark annals
of the Apocrypha.

I wish to sing her praises,
but who hearkens
to the moldering words
of a nameless maid?

EULOGY

From my childhood, I remember
my Aunt Betty, pedestal high
where I put her when I was five,
    where she stayed.

She was my hero, my ideal—
songwriter, poet, sharp words,
warm hugs, brusque and loving,
    mouthpiece of God.

Her wise advice tinted every
major event of my life
and her example made me seek
    a better state of being.

She glowed in the light of laughter
that lifted the sting of grief.
Her loving faith dried tears of pain…
    even her own.

My dear aunt, you who have lived
on love and prayer, now you rest
in the glow of the stars
    that fill your crown.

LUCY—2006-2020

Just a cat—rescued
from abuse, bare patch
on her tail the scar
from her younger life
before she took over
my family.

Alpha Cat slept with dogs,
with me, purred love,
outspoken in meow-talk.
Brought gifts
of mice, lizards, snakes.
Chastised for hunting birds,
being a cat—just a cat.

Gold fur rippled
under strokes,
warm body cuddled on the couch.
Behind green eyes
lay wisdom, intelligence,
an old soul.

Dictator, love bug,
greeter at the door,
adventurer, 24/7
guard-cat, inspector
of my artwork, computer
companion—just a cat.

Just a cat. My cat.
If you've ever
been owned
by a feline person,
you'll understand.

ROBERT (BOB) JOHNSON

You old scoundrel
of the questionable reputation,
colorful language,
a taste for blue humor,
a Molokai man content
to live out your days
as an ex-pat, melding
into a Thai village,
your closest friends the boys
you sponsored and guided
to bright futures.

In your wake flows a stream
of students whom you led
through the intricacies
of English language.
You plastered Facebook
with posts of life past and present,
amusing and pathetic, gleaned
from the internet
by your constant curiosity.
You had no limits
on the help you offered friends
and no patience for those
who didn't meet your standards
of live-and-let-live in this world.

You bearded old goat
in suspenders and plaid cotton shirts,
with a pack of cigarettes in the breast pocket
and your big hairy hugs. . .You were not afraid
to say, "I love you," and I loved you back,
Teacher Bob, my friend.

TAPROOM PHILOSOPHER

Life is a cranky faucet
she mutters around the cigarillo
clenched tight between her teeth.
Water may flow pure and clear,
then the tap burbles and you wonder
if it's over, if this is The End.

She stares down at a broken nail.
Her fuchsia lipstick bleeds
into the brown tobacco stain
at the corner of her mouth.
Sometimes it just burps air
and you think life's empty,

but then with a big gurgle
that faucet lets you know
what it thinks of you—
you hold your hand out to it
and it vomits a mess of rust.
She sighs
sips her beer.

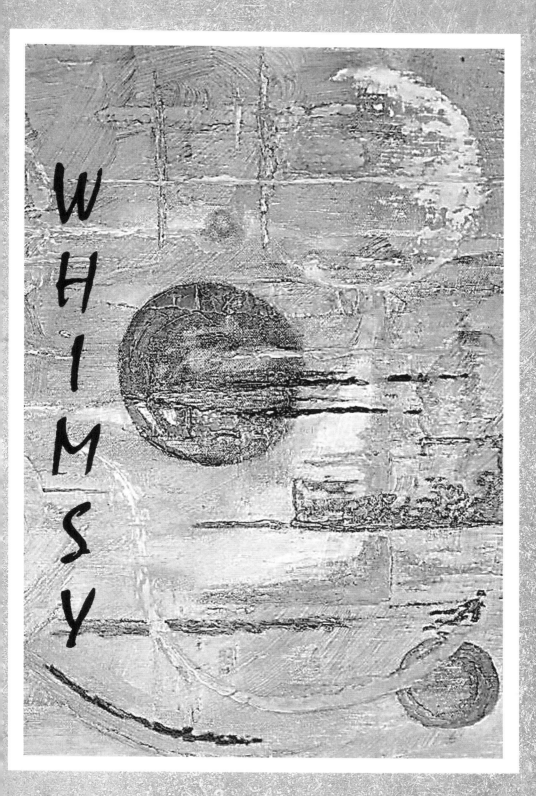

TREASURES

I bought a Dior jacket
in a Thrift Shop.
In Alaska I swirled
a pan of gravel under the spout,
caught the sparkle of flecks of gold
among the pebbles.

At a mine I sat in mud,
dug through piles
of discarded red dirt, discovered
a perfect crystal which cast
a rainbow onto my palm.

From a class of "too-cool-to-care"
students I receive, years later,
letters of gratitude and success.

Life teems with hidden treasures
—joy in the unexpected.

NO FORGIVENESS

I cannot say that you and I
had 40 years of bliss.
However, any minor tiffs
were smoothed with a drink and a kiss.

We led a life of excitement and fun
of travel and duty and stress
fulfilling the diplomatic role
required by *oblige noblesse.*

You catered with copious spirits
I provided the *haute cuisine.*
The next day you'd be comatose
needing lashings of caffeine.

Never mind, we staggered on with life.
I forgave your love of booze.
You were smart and witty, faithful to me
...one can't always pick and choose!

With high life and liquor and dinners galore
you became increasingly stout.
Your heart developed a flutter,
your foot, a case of gout.

It's not that I was the perfect wife
but you were always forgiving
and looking back, I cannot think
of a better way of living.

So I thank you for a wonderful time
lived to the Nth degree.
But I cannot forgive your final act—
you went and died on me.

BP

The doctor calls it "Blood Pressure."
I call it Life Pressure.

When my brain
is whirling, twisting,
bouncing here and there,
my blood gets all excited,
starts galumphing
through those
skinny vessels,
pushing
shoving.

Perhaps the systolic
is only an IQ score.

BETTER TO BE 31

At thirty, when my birthday came,
refused to be delayed,
it mercilessly pulled me from
the "Still there's time" decade.
I faced an unknown image,
trembled to behold
that strange and sad identity—
Child-Prodigy-Grown-Old.

A year I had to break the strands
my youthful dreams had spun
and bind myself to middle age.
I enjoyed 31.

NIGHTGUARD MELODY

My dreams change
when I sleep in my nightguard.
I am competent, important.
I flash my plastic smile
as I plan a major wedding reception
in a venue vaguely resembling
a cross between La Scala
and the Super Bowl arena.

I welcome guests
to my mansion, place friends
and a few strangers into rooms
lavishly decorated, each sporting
a well-stocked bar, while horses whinny
in the stables outside.

The dentist says I grind my teeth.
I don't know about that, I am asleep,
but I try to remember
to wear the guard to protect
these brave survivors of ice
cubes, jaw breakers, ears of corn
and peanut brittle.

Most of my teeth aren't real
but they're mine—I paid dearly
for these crowns and implants.
The only "originals" are my lower
front teeth, now seventy-five years old
and worn down like a horse's dentition.

I need a "dayguard" for my brain
to keep it in line and protect it
when worries start grinding.

A WARNING

This is my sincere warning of
an ever-present threat—
a caution that your past may hold
events you should forget.
It is the current rage to delve
in genealogy
designing Family Trees through charts
and new histology

but lurking in your DNA
are herds of blackened sheep—
do you really want to focus on
the secrets that they keep?!
Why choose to change your happy song
into a threnody?
Did your relative shoot Lincoln, Lennon,
even Kennedy?

When looking up that dear old man
known as Uncle Pappy
Who needs to know that it was little
boys that made him happy?
That branch in Arkansas is one
entangled inbred mass.
Your most-revered ancestor later
died from...something crass.

Those cattle-rustlers, thieves and cads,
disgraced in years gone by,
molesters, liars, killers-all...
just leave it—let them lie
in a cloud of past-unknown,
remain a mystery.
I warn you it's a dangerous game,
exhuming history.

WHAT IF?

She's gone from me, my Crissi-girl,
my lovely little Griff.
I'm left with tears, an ache in my heart,
and the haunting thought, *What if?*

What if I'd kept her closer to me?
Made the years roll away?
But useless contemplation
won't heal my grief today.
For every time I say, *What if?*
I know there's another side—
What if she'd never been rescued
to become my joy, my pride?

The light in her deep brown eyes showed trust.
She could make me smile
through my sadness, stress, or pain
if I held her for a while.
When I came home and opened the door,
she barked in ecstasy.
I got kisses every morning
when she lay next to me.

Say that she's crossed the Rainbow Bridge;
  call it a blessed' release;
    call it the end of a loving life...
Now my Crissi is at peace.

FELINE FECUNDITY

Dedicated to our feral cat Dirty Nose,
whom we 'tamed' with handouts when
she was a few months old and pregnant.

Little cat with dirty nose,
your amber, slitted eyes search mine
for comfort? guidance? goodness knows...

Your kitten brain can't comprehend
nature's premature design
that brought your youth to such an end.

You've lost your playfulness, your purr,
splayed are your legs and swayed your spine,
you bulge with smudged and rippling fur.

Think, when next you wish to mate—
when kittens with a Tom entwine...
this rotund malady's your fate:

Decline!

COMPUTER ILLITERACY

Technology
      chews up my hours
      spits them out
      in mangled minutes

The debris
      spreads across the day
      —a dark cloud that obscures
      inspiration, necessity
      responsibilities

The poem
      that hovered
      at the edge of my thoughts
      lies wrinkled and dry
      ...advanced *rigor mortis*

I should consult a ten-year-old!

LEFTOVERS

I ate the last of your yogurt today,
appropriately chilled.
Catkins and mulberries
punctuate the terrace
where we sat
in plastic Adirondack chairs
on the first warm day
before spring. The willow wore
only a green haze of promise,
like our relationship
which we explored
sipping cooled coffee.

Last night, at midnight
I sat on that terrace,
heard one mockingbird
aping his avian kin in trills
shrieks and clicks,
saw the moon wink
through passing clouds.
Gotcha!
he seemed to say.

Oh, and you left
one blue sock
under the bed.

POEM MISSING?

It is not a mistake.

You have not missed the poem
due to appear on this page.
It is still in my head—somewhere.

Perhaps I can shake it loose with a Cowboy Two-Step
across the living room; or smooth its edges
with a glass of wine, so it slips out;
or sing a sultry song

to call it forth; or read a few chapters of Ulysses
so it becomes frustrated
with the company it's keeping
and begs to come out.

On the other hand, perhaps
it is cowering in a corner, surrounded
by dinner menus, visitors, hungry dogs,

and dirty dishes. Perhaps it will pull
an empty metaphor
over its head and expire.

I'll keep searching, cajoling,
pondering on the vastness
of a field of words waiting to be harvested
and rolled into a neat round bale of poetry.

I am bereft of inspiration
but competently coping
with leftovers and soap suds.

SENILITY RAP

If I stop to count the years,
then I'm over many hills—
post-menopausal, and drenched in pills
with rheumatism coming and my eyesight going,
my boobs both sagging and my grey hair showing.

I'm mature and mastodonic, a creaky chronic sample
of a breed almost extinct.

I wear a vest in winter and Thrift Store clothes.
I seldom go to dances or to fashion shows.
I like Old Time Religion, and I love my ma
but I wear bikini briefs and a see-through bra.

I'm a tyro-mystic, anachronistic, masochistic madam
of a breed almost extinct.

I still connect Madonna to the virgin birth.
My stuff is all in storage
and my daughter lives in Perth.
My most exciting turn-on
is the switch on my computer
but I 'm a dual-national and a jet commuter,

a near-neurotic, half-psychotic semiotic scholar
of a breed almost extinct.

It's been a quarter century since I kissed a guy—
I recall it was exciting, but I can't remember why.
Somewhere in my psyche runs a soul
that's young and gay,
and a poetry reviewer called my work risqué.

I'm a twist and shouting, faith and doubting,
curbed and spouting female
of a breed almost extinct.

A LAST LAUGH

Online Shopper

I keep buying bras
hoping for uplift.
Perhaps I should employ
a rope and pulley device
Helium injections
a backhoe.

Friendship

Friendship is precious—
important like no other.
Treasure it, revere your friend,
except when she wants your lover.

À La Dorothy Parker

Senior status frees me from
the need to please mankind.
These days I'm neither green nor dumb
I govern my own mind.

I rule my roost, no man or mouse
ruffles my plumes awry.
So, come on up to my chicken house,
if you're man enough to try!

Convergences

SEE SPOT RUN

I was obnoxious
in the first grade.
Having been reading
interesting stories for
two or three years,
I thought Dick and Jane
were totally lame.

As a woman of a Certain Age
clinging to my cognitive functions
with Prevagen and push-ups,
I note that aging requires
ever-increasing reading of small print,
bottom lines, and documents
phrased in gobbledygook.

With synapses less snappy
attention span decimated
and polysyllabic words
disappearing from my discourse
I think fondly
of Dick and Jane.

FOR YOU, MY DAUGHTER

In my paperchain of memories
many links are broken,
but I treasure that chain
as it flutters down
the corridors of years.

So many of the brightest links—
the most colorful connections,
strong gold circles that hold firm,
silver ellipses that sparkle—
are those fashioned by you.

You are the decoration of my days
the link that draws me home
the symbol of a life
that is not without continuity
because there is you.

RIVERS

You can never step into the same river twice;
for other waters are ever flowing on to you.
                        —*Heraclitus*

Boxes surround me
stacked high.
I find my mother's journal
from 1932, joyful descriptions
of summer Sunday picnics
with friends by the river.

Returning to the banks
of the Little Sugar river,
in that green country
where we both began
I search the flow for an image
of Mother, a laughing young woman
on her picnic blanket.

Minnows dart beneath me,
ripples climb the stones,
break into bubbles
that the current consumes
and rushes on without recollection
of my young white toes
that once wriggled in the shallows.

Waters rising from the springs
of my heart overflow.
Each tear carries its story
downstream, out of sight,
with no memory of its passage.

EDMOND MEMORIES

I was eight when we moved to Edmond.
I remember red canna lilies
around Old North, the centerpiece
of Central State College, it was then.
Those flowers are gone, along with
two former libraries. The presidents lived
in a red brick house on campus
across from Thompson's Book Store,
and Quonsets provided extra student housing.
Everyone I knew was from college
or church, or both.

I remember my first kiss
one Sunday, among the sand and bags
of cement under the skeleton staircase
on the construction site. I was 11 or 12.
A boy and I crossed the street
from church to look at our new
Sunday School, or was it the auditorium?
Terrible how my memory's gone
but I remember his name—
Gerald Brookhouse Getter III.

Mother and Daddy were married
in that church, then 20 years later
Richard and I. Nicki was born,
Richard and Daddy died.
I dropped in to visit over the years.
Mother had a reception at the BSU on campus
when my British diplomat and Nicki and I
came through, before Dublin, after Pakistan.
Everyone came—can't remember who.

Terrible how my memory's gone, but I remember
a sense of rejection when I discovered
the college had thrown out my placement file.
I guess they thought I was placed.

Gallons of water have passed
under the bridge. Some of it ran
into tears, but much went to irrigate
good crops that produced
some beautiful harvests. Perhaps
it's the combination that teaches us
how to cross the current with the flow.
Tears and sweat and sunshine
make the river, and it has carried me
where I didn't know I was meant to go.

Central's a university now and I
am an aging poet and teacher
and my dog is getting old. Many things
I can't remember, but people and places
glue my life together, and I find
a kind of security in seeing the world
from where it began.

The local newspaper reported
She has gone far...and come back.
What an epitaph!

YOUTH, GONE AWAY

Looking back, through the decades of life's later day
I remember my youth, gone away, gone away.

Then there was in the venture a kindred aim,
a common hope, a world to blame
for the blindness and deafness, the plodding way
that held, New-World-pinioned, that youth,
gone astray.

Then there lay in the future life's wheel to spin,
a star to touch, a goal to win,
and I trembled, impatient with time's delays
while I planned how to pattern that youth's
better days.

Then there came in the struggle a dream wrung dry,
a wearied hope, a chance passed by.
Then the point of the effort became but to stay
on the wheel, while the freshness of youth
spun away.

So that in the revolving cycles of years
within the spin of Time's cold spheres
I listen for whispers of dreams gone astray—
hear only the echoes of youth, far away.

Weeks turn to decades. Years flee so fast
spinning and spinning through scenes of the past.
Tomorrow's intentions become past regret.
No sooner does day dawn, than evening is set.

I am that I am that I am...only this.
Pain often intrudes on our memories of bliss
and what is recalled at our Moment of Truth
is the dream of that far-away, faded youth.

UNHEARD CONTEMPLATIONS

My dog has lost her hearing.
She sits, head cocked,
listening for what—
for my voice
for the backyard cacophony
of birds, barking, distant cars,
whisper of leaves?

So much is lost, not to be found—
time, youth, loved ones.
Railway stations and department stores
maintain optimism with their collections
of "Lost and Found," implying
the possibility of recovery. *Seek
and ye shall find*...occasionally.

I have lost family, pets,
years, sometimes hope.
I have lost husbands, yet I cling
to my Christian credenda, the promise
that love is not lost but waits
to be found...beyond.

SUN CHILD

I was a sun-child
before *Melanoma* entered my vocabulary
July at the swimming hole in Arkansas
turned my young skin
from sallow white
to walnut brown.
The sign of a successful summer
was the depth of tan displayed
to friends when school began
in the fall.

I basked, years later, under a tropical sky,
where waves crashed over the reef,
sang as they threaded through
antler coral, whispered
as they ran onto white sand,
upending busy crabs, redesigned
tide patterns on the beach,
and consumed a child's sandcastle
before ebbing.

Another beach, another sky,
beside another sea, I stretched
on fine-grain sand, closed
my eyes against the searing sun.
I lay in happy contentment
amidst the murmur of tide,
rustle of palm fronds,
rapid-fire native language
drowned at intervals
by motorcycle roar.

With the taste of salt
on my lips, I breathed the smell
of seaweed, fish, charcoal fires
roasting *satay*, Eastern
spices and Western sweat.
When the sun began
to burn my toes,
I burrowed them into deeper sand,
in the cool damp
where tiny sea creatures hide.

Through slitted eyes
the silhouette of a fishing boat
against a stark blue sky
gave me pleasure in the knowledge
that this place—the gentle sea,
tin and tiled roofs along the shore
behind the palm tree sentinels—
always gave me perfect moments.

The sea, the years, the tan
have gone. My dermatologist
tsks in disapproval
of my long ago love affair
with the sun.

RELEASE

Swirling images are peopled by
her shadow and the feeble ghost of one
who set domestic traps upon her path
with his expressions of pathetic love
and gratitude, requiring her to act
as lover, mother, counselor, without
the consolation of security.

That world, that home, that patriarchy
stunned her soul, her inspiration; led her
from the healing respite for her inner self
of poetry and art. She floundered deep
in quagmires of society's façades.
Dark corners of rare solitude were filled
with echoes of a distant voice, a cry

that rode on wind and stretched the sound
to occupy each corner of her pain
but only when she covered her ears
did she understand that the wailing
was her own. It rose in mounting decibels
and found release in written words, set down
in testament of a new resolve.

Today she dines alone on less than *Cordon Bleu*
and lives in rooms not quite as grand.
Her friends believe her life has been a whirl
of great excitement, travel through the world,
a constant stream of magnates, kings, and stars.
She smiles and clutches secrets to her heart.
Erato whispers poems in her dreams.

MY COUNTRY 'TIS OF ME

I drive to the earthquakes every morning
on borrowed wheels and stolen time,
feel the heave and shake
of torn core, exposed roots,
watch the rim of the abyss
crumble slowly toward my feet.

Let those who trash the world
clean it up. Me—
I wait for my exit
over the edge.

NIGHT VISIONS

Midsummer nights bring memory,
dreams of sunlight on white lotus,
whispers of the ebbing tide,
vibrations of the temple bell
that shakes loose visions
in my mind.

Noontime rays thread
drooping Poinciana leaves,
pattern the dust where children play.
Ring-a ring of roses a pocket full...
hands joined, they dance in circles,
fade.

Empty schoolyard. Moonlight
strokes the Buddha on the hill.
In the house my friend sleeps
behind the night.
Farewell is a perilous word,
better left unspoken.

Dawn rises
through shadows of clouds.
The dream splits,
reveals its cold hard core
of reality, spreads the chill
of manufactured air.

HIS DREAM DEFERRED

We are all leaves of one tree.
We are all waves of one sea.
—Thich Nhat Hanh
1926-2022

Gnarled wood groans
beneath the weight
of sorrow and dissension

One by one
withered leaves break
from the branches

The "shining sea"
recedes, grows dull
crusts with brine

Not even the moon
can lift waves
folded in on themselves

No longer
one tree   one sea
gentle mindfulness

Animosity obscures
the peaceful path
of unity

FLOWING

Slouched in the recliner
I take my pulse,
count miniature jumps
of the coffee cup on my chest—
72 per minute.
Not dead.

Alive, but caught in the flow
of the Keepers of Time.
Mind and body are prisoners
of the years. Incarceration
sucks the juices that fuel
the power to swim
against the current.

The mighty tree of my ambition
lies uprooted on the bank.
I cling to an overhanging branch,
resist the flow, think a poem,
dodge the debris.

MY WISH FOR YOU

I wish you
sun rise and full moons
bright stars and blue skies
music in your heart
  and quiet in your soul
the luxuries of living
  and a poverty of care
God's concern
  and your lack of it
mornings full of promise
  and evenings laced in satisfaction
a loving heart
great joy
and the intoxication
  of tranquility.

A BIT ABOUT ME

I am a retired dual-national, now living in Oklahoma City. My occupation and pre-occupation are with my artist daughter and rescued Brussels Griffon dog, plus writing, volunteering for the blind, Tai Chi-ing, traveling, and visiting with friends. Life is good.

Most of my adult life was spent outside the United States, as a teacher and as a British diplomatic wife. Recent travel restrictions and retirement have allowed me to revisit the journals and photographs from those years. Between the yellowed lines of writings and behind the fading pictures, I find experiences and emotions to be recalled and savored.

Inspired by my poetry critique groups and online peepholes into life around me, I continue to write poetry. I write to preserve memories; I write to explore thoughts and feelings; I write because that is how I process life.

Performing my poems gives me pleasure because I feel the music of our language swells when a poem is read aloud.

As former American Laureate Robert Pinskey said, *If a poem is written well, it was written with the poet's voice and for a voice. Reading a poem silently...is like the difference between staring at sheet music and actually humming or playing the music on an instrument.*

I hope you like humming my songs.

Judith

jsrycroft@yahoo.com